The
Parable
of the
Perfect
Parent

Edward H. West, MD

ISBN 979-8-88751-025-5 (paperback)
ISBN 979-8-88751-026-2 (digital)

Christian Faith Publishing
832 Park Avenue
Meadville, PA 16335
www.christianfaithpublishing.com

Printed in the United States of America

"A son honors his father; and a servant his master.
Then if I am a father, where is My honor? And if I am a
master, where is My respect?" says the Lord of hosts.

—Malachi 1:6 (NAS)

God is always the Lord, the ultimate owner and authority. All His ways are perfect.

To Christian believers, God is also "our Father, who art in heaven" (Matthew 6:9 NAS). He is the Father who knows us intimately. He desires such a close relationship with us that He urges us to call Him "Daddy!"

God is our model of the perfect parent.

The Old Testament tells the story of God and the nation of Israel. God works with the nation, just as a father deals with his sometimes wayward child.

The Old Testament might be a parable of the wise father of a child who wants to go his own way.

The New Testament reveals God as the perfect Father of Jesus, His perfect Son. The relationship between the divine Father and Son is eternally perfect, as the will of the Father is always precisely the will of the Son.

We are the adopted children of God. Often, we fail to conform to the will of our Father. We are imperfect, just as our own children are imperfect.

So the parable of the perfect parent could be about God, your perfect parent, who works in your life as a father, bringing you to maturity. It could also speak to you as a parent, showing you how to deal with your own child when your wills do not align.

Because we are imperfect, our understanding of our Father's will and intentions is incomplete. We depend on God; we need intimacy with Him to receive the full benefits of His love. However, we are self-determining individuals who want to be in charge of our own lives.

God's fatherhood requires that He maintain the authority of a teacher and leader. He must deal with our willfulness while walking beside us like a father who cherishes us. God has told us about our destiny:

> "For those whom He foreknew, He also predestined to become conformed to the image of his Son."

> —Romans 8:29 (NAS)

As His adopted children, He intends that we become like Jesus and join His family.

God loves us before we are born with a father's rich, tender love. His love is not based on a need that we must supply. To Him, we are a special treasure to teach and to enjoy.

God watches over us constantly and wants to actively participate in our lives. He wants us to really know Him and learn to imitate His character and conduct. He wants His values to be ours.

His loving attention so obviously confirms how valuable we are that we begin to value ourselves. The pleasure that our company gives Him strengthens us to face the challenges ahead.

I have loved you with an everlasting love; therefore
I have drawn you with lovingkindness.

—Jeremiah 31:3 (NAS)

Like children, we have nothing to contribute to this relationship except ourselves. We are totally dependent on God. His love irresistibly draws us to Him, and we look to our Father to provide for us.

How precious is Your loving kindness,
O God! And the children of men take refuge in the shadow
of Your wings. They drink their fill of the abundance of Your
house; and You give them to drink of the river of Your delights.

—Psalm 36:7–8 (NAS)

In life, there is safety and danger; there is right and wrong. God knows what we do not know. He has the wisdom to direct us in the right way. God gives us wisdom in the form of rules. His rules reflect His values, the principles that are most important to Him.

He is careful not to overwhelm us with endless regulations. His rules are carefully designed for our good.

I will instruct you and teach you in the way which you
should go; I will counsel you with My eye upon you.

—Psalm 32:8 (NAS)

With His rules, He challenges us to submit to His authority and agree that He is in charge. If we *listen*—that is, if we hear, understand, and obey Him—we will learn wisdom.

Our impulse to love Him in return is expressed primarily by simply accepting His love and submitting to His authority. When we obey His rules and walk with Him, we show our love for Him.

Your ears will hear a word behind you, "This is the way, walk in it," whenever you turn to the right or to the left.

—Isaiah 30:21 (NAS)

When we agree that God is in charge and listen to Him, we display the good attitude of a disciple toward his teacher. A disciple is a student who learns by doing the teaching.

As disciples, we continuously practice the proper alignment with our Father, so we can fully benefit from His discipline. Discipline is learning by practicing. We learn wisdom—the right way to go—from our Father, our teacher.

Only when we are willing to be disciples can we really be disciplined.

Teach me Your way, O Lord; I will walk in Your
truth; unite my heart to fear Your name.

—Psalm 86:11 (NAS)

Because we have a good attitude and listen to God, a close relationship can flourish.

With time, we more deeply understand who our Father really is—the One who loves us beyond reason and who directs us by His rules in the way of wisdom. This understanding leads us to truly "honor" Him (that is, to give careful consideration and then behave accordingly).

As we honor Him and listen to Him, His values become ours. Our walk together is intimate.

By this we know that we have come to know
Him, if we keep His commandments.

—1 John 2:3 (NAS)

We are not in a relationship of equality with God. Because He is Lord, He has a superior status and is rightfully in charge. His authority (that is, His capacity to command obedience) is supported by dominating power, which He's willing to use if necessary.

Because of who He is, our Father can and should tell us what to do. When God states a rule, He marks the path of wisdom. He wants us to agree that He is in charge and to go the right way. If we do not listen, disobedience results.

Disobedience reveals our self-centered nature, which causes us to want to be in charge and challenge God's authority. It interferes with His work as a father.

How can He raise us to maturity without our honor? How can He have an intimate relationship without our respect?

God responds to our disobedience like a patient, loving, and wise father. His purpose is reconciliation.

Thus says the Lord, "Stand by the ways and see and ask for the ancient paths, where the good way is, and walk in it; and you will find rest for your souls." But they said, "We will not walk in it."

—Jeremiah 6:16 (NAS)

These are reasons for our misbehavior:

1. We cannot behave correctly due to physical or emotional factors.
2. We do not know or understand the rule and so misbehave unintentionally.
3. We are not practiced in following the rule and misbehave from a lack of self-control.
4. We oppose the idea that God is in charge, develop a bad attitude toward God's authority, and misbehave out of rebellion.

Any of these possibilities could explain an incident of misbehavior. Sometimes, there is more than one explanation.

God considers the reasons for our misbehavior, carefully searching for a motive.

For the Lord is a God of knowledge, and
with Him actions are weighed.

—1 Samuel 2:3 (NAS)

God corrects us according to our individual insight, abilities, limitations, and intentions. He simply instructs us if that is sufficient. If we are true disciples, He trains us to practice self-control and go the right way.

For whom the Lord loves He reproves, even as a
father corrects the son in whom he delights.

—Proverbs 3:12 (NAS)

But when misbehavior arises from a bad attitude, the attitude, not the misbehavior, is the critical issue. God is particularly strict on this point. He expects obedience but will not tolerate a bad attitude.

God wants a father's relationship with us. Such intimacy requires that we honor Him, acknowledging the difference in status between God and ourselves. It also requires that we cheerfully agree with Him to go the right way, having the proper attitude of a disciple.

When we object to His being in charge, the intimacy of our parent-child relationship is threatened. We no longer respect Him for who He is. We are no longer disciples, so we resist discipline. We refuse to listen, so we do not hear instructions.

A bad attitude is a disaster. Reconciliation is mandatory.

Listen, O heavens, and hear, O earth; for the Lord speaks, "Sons I have reared and brought up, but they have revolted against Me."

—Isaiah 1:2 (NAS)

When we deliberately choose to go the wrong way, our intimacy with God is broken because He cannot go that way. With a bad attitude, we wander away from the companionship of God and into the misery of self-imposed isolation.

During this time, God is silent, but He continues to care for us and tend to our needs. Perhaps He stirs a longing for the joy of the intimacy now lost. Eventually, the stress of isolation causes us to review our disastrous decision.

God can wait longer than we can.

Then they will cry out to the Lord, but He will not answer them. Instead, He will hide His face from them at that time because they have practiced evil deeds.

—Micah 3:4 (NAS)

In isolation, we find that we miss our Father and long for His company. Since it was our decision that led to our bad attitude in the relationship, it is left to us to decide the next step.

To restore intimacy, we must change our attitude. Realigning and returning to God can be accomplished only through sincere confession, apology, and repentance. God will not participate in a dishonest attempt. We must be sincerely sorry and committed to an honest reconciliation that accepts His superior status, or we will remain in isolation.

With the pure You show Yourself pure, and with
the perverted You show Yourself astute.

—2 Samuel 22:27 (NAS)

When we come to our senses, our awareness of His constant love and the permanence of His fatherhood urges us to return and be reconciled. We agree with Him that we were wrong. We seek His forgiveness for rebelling against His authority. We believe He will forgive us and wants to resume a father's role as our teacher and leader.

God's forgiveness is profound and complete. He never stopped loving us. He never stopped being our Father.

Just as a father has compassion on his children, so the Lord
has compassion on those who fear Him. For He Himself
knows our frame; He is mindful that we are but dust.

—Psalm 103:13–14 (NAS)

With intimacy restored, God can resume the task of instructing and training us. Because we have a proper attitude, we accept His discipline as an expression of love, not as punishment.

Often, there are consequences of misbehavior that are natural and logical. As disciples, we accept the consequences and learn from them. Sometimes, our Father's tender love leads Him to spare us consequences. When we have a proper attitude, we recognize this as God's mercy rather than a sign of weakness. With intimacy restored, whether facing the consequences or appreciating mercy, we know His decisions are for our good.

After reconciliation, God restates the rule. This time, if we have really learned who He is and how to listen, we will go with Him in the right way, enjoying Him as children enjoy their father.

But He knows the way I take; when He has tried me,
I shall come forth as gold. My foot has held fast to His
path; I have kept His way and not turned aside.

—Job 23:10–11 (NAS)

God values us far beyond our apparent worth and wants to enjoy our companionship. He is intimately involved in our concerns and wants to give us what we most desire. It is God who gives us our own children and a hope for their future. Someday, we must give an accounting to Him concerning ourselves and the gifts He has entrusted to us.

God is the perfect parent. He shows us how to raise our children wisely and gives us the power to raise them well.

We are imperfect parents under construction. We look to God as our model and as our source of power.

Therefore be imitators of God, as beloved children.

—Ephesians 5:1 (NAS)

PLAN A and PLAN B

If a parable is an earthly story with a heavenly meaning, then in story after story, and book after book, the Old Testament is a parable of God, the Perfect Parent, and His rebellious child, the nation of Israel. The parable is spoken in countless ways through many authors. Here is one summary:

> Listen, my people, to my instruction; incline your ears to the words of my mouth. I will open my mouth in a parable; I will tell riddles of old, which we have heard and known, and our fathers have told us. We will not conceal them from their children, but we will tell the generation to come the praises of the Lord, and His power and His wondrous works that He has done. For He has established a testimony in Jacob, and appointed a law in Israel, which He commanded our fathers that they were to teach them to their children, so that the generations to come would know, the children yet to be born, that they would arise and tell them to their children, so that they would put their confidence in God, and not forget the works of God, but comply with His commandments, and not be like their fathers, a stubborn and rebellious generation that did not prepare its heart and whose spirit was not faithful to God.
>
> —Psalm 78:1-8 (NAS)

PLAN A and PLAN B

The Father of Israel had plans for His child. There was a plan for when the child listened and a plan for when he resisted:

> "For I know the plans I have for you," says the Lord, "plans for welfare and not for calamity to give you a future and a hope."
>
> —Jeremiah 29:11 (NAS)

The Old Testament is a long, complicated narrative with many twists and turns. But the parable is a shining, simple path and the plans of God for His child are simple. The two paths, that someday join, are "Plan A" and "Plan B."

PLAN A

"For I know the plans that I have for you," declares the Lord, "plans for your welfare...to give you a future."
— Jeremiah 29:11

"So choose life...by loving the Lord your God, by obeying His voice and by holding fast to Him."
— Deuteronomy 30:19-20

"And I said, 'you shall call Me, "My Father," and not turn away from following me.'"
— Jeremiah 3:19

"I am Thy servant; give me understanding." — Psalm 119:125

PLAN B

"According to their transgressions, I dealt with them."
— Ezekiel 39:24

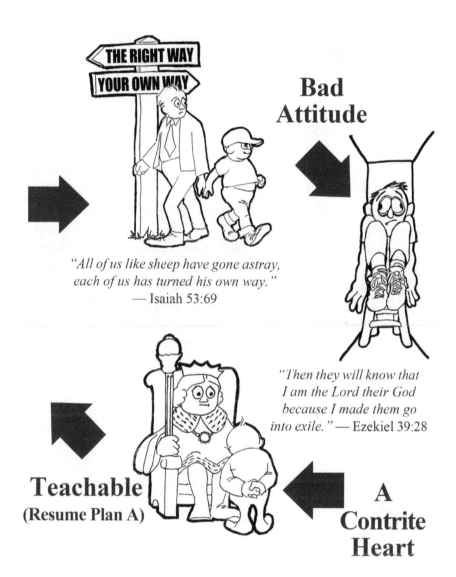

Bad Attitude

"All of us like sheep have gone astray, each of us has turned his own way."
— Isaiah 53:69

"Then they will know that I am the Lord their God because I made them go into exile." — Ezekiel 39:28

Teachable
(Resume Plan A)

A Contrite Heart

"And I said, 'I will confess my transgressions to the Lord; and Thou didst forgive the guilt of my sin'" — Psalm 32:5

About the Author

Ed West is a father, a Bible teacher, and a physician who retired after a career of almost forty years in general pediatrics in his native South Carolina. He has years of experience in family counseling and teaching biblical child-rearing, often outside of American culture. He teaches the wisdom of the Bible to hopeful parents who accept the truth of scripture.

He shares with the apostle Paul a concern that in the last days, the gospel message of the power of God will be diluted by teachers, and the apostasy of the end-times will follow because men will be "holding to a form of godliness, although they have denied its power" (2 Timothy 3:5 NAS). His message is that bringing a child to maturity requires that the child change and that, because parents are the teachers charged with this critical work, they must change (mature) ahead of their children.

Printed in the USA
CPSIA information can be obtained
at www.ICGtesting.com
LVHW021957090224
771275LV00002B/106